Santa wants a makeover by Monica & Ekta

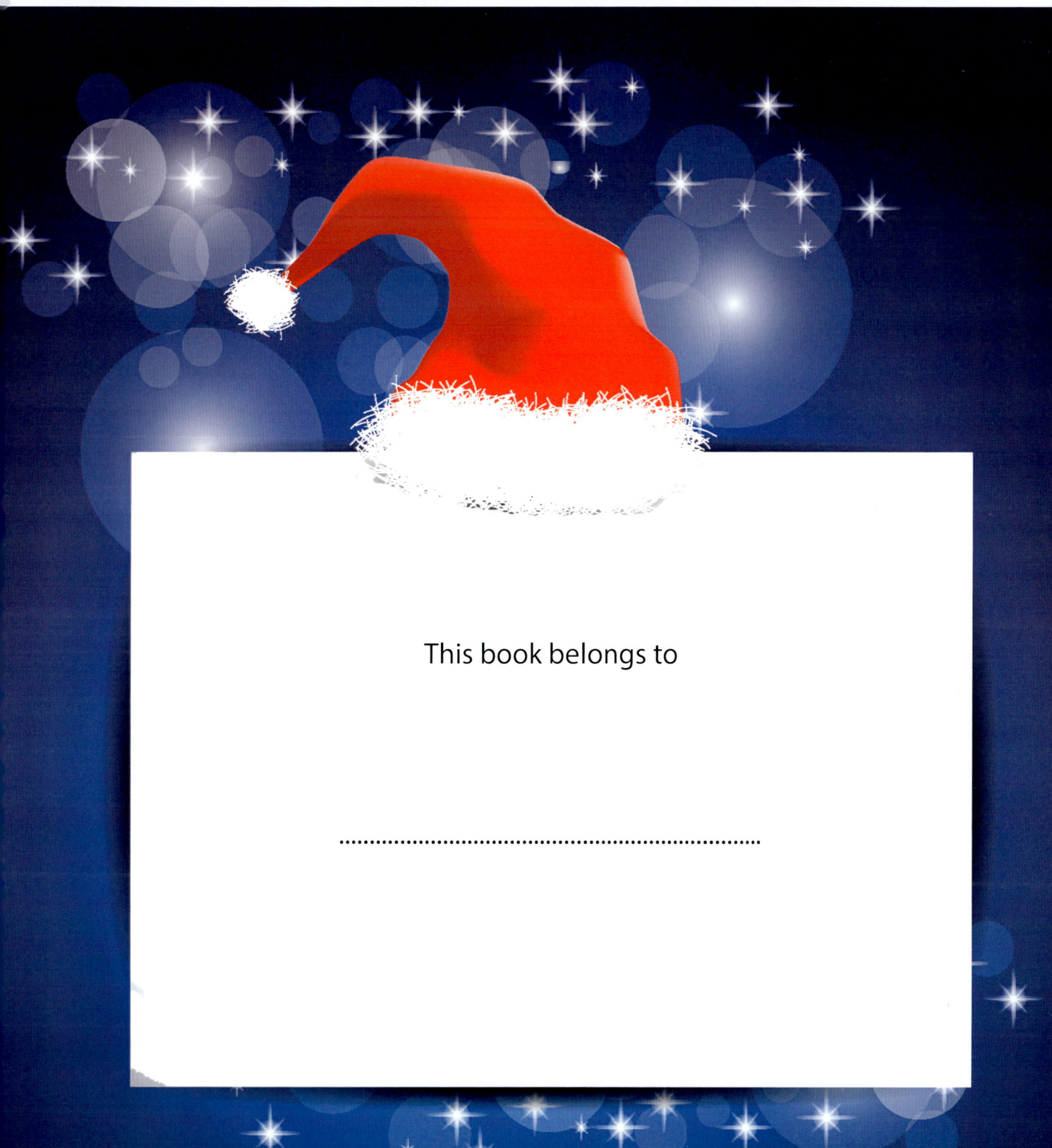
This book belongs to

....

Christmas is just days away,

Ten keen reindeers jump- hooray!

Nine elves run to work in haste,

There was no time for them to waste.

Seven times, he knocks on old oak door,

Peeping through the window, he gets to know more.

Santa's red coat is lying on the chair,
Mrs Claus looks in tremendous despair.
Six different outfits lay on the floor,
Reindeers and elves look very unsure.

Elf the postman quickly takes over,

When Mrs Clause whispers,

"Santa wants a makeover."

Hastily, the reindeers design **five** pair of shoes,

But Santa looks too confused to choose.

The elves stitched **four** new hats,
White like snow and soft like a cuddly cat.
All the guests cheered wow!
But Santa was not pleased somehow.

Three different looks are then tried,
But Santa seems disappointed inside.

Quietly, Santa walks away to his room. Everyone thinks that Christmas is doomed. HO! HO! HO! Santa comes out with **one** loud cheer, His new look surprises everyone there.

Mrs Claus whispers in Santa's ear,
'You look **perfect**, my dear."
This is the look that children have loved so far,
You look the best the way you are!

Everyone cheers,
Hip, Hip Hooray!
Santa, along with his reindeers' whizz on the sleigh...

ME SERIES, compiled and designed by
Monica and Ekta

Published by Author In Me
@2016, High Wycombe
www.authorinme.com

Copyright © Author In Me Ltd 2016

All rights reserved. No part of this publication may be reproduced, stored in a retrieval system or transmitted, in any form or by any means, electronic, mechanical, photocopying, recording or otherwise, without the prior permission of the copyright holder.

Printed in UK